Your *BRILLIANT*
CAREER GOALS

A 6-step plan to find out what you REALLY want to do – whether you want to do something completely different, have reached a career crossroads, or want to check you are going in the right direction.

By

Anna Sheather

Published by Élan Coaching Ltd

www.elancoaching.co.uk

Book cover design by Spiffing Covers Ltd

First published 2015

ISBN: 978-1-910667-41-5

ISBN: 978-1-910667-42-2 (.mobi)

ISBN: 978-1-910667-43-9 (.epub)

Already out there

Your *Brilliant* CV

Coming Soon

Your *Brilliant* Interview
Your *Brilliant* Covering Letters & Emails
Your *Brilliant* Transferable Skills
Your *Brilliant* Job Search
Your *Brilliant* Application Form
Your *Brilliant* Confidence

Contents

INTRODUCTION

Having coached a wide variety of people at all stages of their careers, I have decided to put my fingers to the keyboard to share my experiences with you. My clients have come from all walks of life, different industry sectors and different stages of their careers, from first-time workers through to Chief Executives of multimillion-pound organisations. Many have suggested that I write books, so I have finally given in and done just that!

This booklet is part of the *'Your Brilliant...'* series. I have written this series for anyone who is looking for advice and guidance on getting and securing their next role, whether it is their first role, a complete change of career direction or the next step on their career path. Each booklet covers a specific career-coaching topic and has been written this way so that you can pick and choose the support you need for your own career-coaching requirements. Each booklet is designed for you to work through and coach yourself to career success!

I hope you will find this booklet helpful, and any others in the series that you use.

Introduction to *'Your Brilliant Career Goals'*

People often come to me when they are at some form of crossroads in their career or working life.

They want to:

- do something different but just don't know what
- reignite their interest in work as they have stagnated, got bored and aren't enjoying work any more
- take advantage of the opportunities being made redundant has given them – opportunities to change their career or working life and do what they really want to do
- explore opportunities at work and decide what they want to do next

The first question I ask is do they have a goal in mind? To which the answer is invariably no. Some have a few thoughts but have no idea how to get there or whether what they want to do is realistic and/or achievable. Some people laugh and say '*I know what I'd **really** like to do but...*' already limiting their career goals. If this sounds like you, then this booklet is for you!

In this booklet I have set out my approach to helping people like you work out exactly what they want to do, helping them put together a realistic, practical career goal and, in the final chapter, getting them started on their journey.

I hope this booklet helps you find where you want to go, whether you are starting out in your career, have reached a career crossroads or want to check you are going in the right direction.

Before you dip in, please read Chapter 1 - Getting the best from this booklet.

Good luck!

Anna

CHAPTER 1
GETTING THE BEST FROM THIS BOOKLET

This booklet has been written as a workbook to help you think through what you **really** want from your working life.

This workbook is for you if you:

- have no idea what you want to do

- know you want to do something different but are not sure what

- have just set out on your career and want to make sure you are making the right decisions about your job choices

- have opportunities at work but are not sure if they are right for you

- know what you want to do but are struggling to get started

- already have some idea about your goal and want to check you are going in the right direction.

This booklet contains exercises, questionnaires and ideas that will help you to:

- be honest with yourself about what you really want to do and why

- understand what motivates you in your career

- understand the importance of your values and beliefs in having a fulfilled working life

- check that your career goal is **really** yours and not someone else's!

- research your thoughts and ideas to come up with realistic options and choices about what you want to do

- work out your career goal and write it in a realistic, practical and achievable way

- get you started on the road to success.

When doing these exercises, it is important to realise that it is only you who can identify what you want to do; I cannot do that for you. You are the expert in you. I can help facilitate your thinking, providing you with tools to help you unlock what you already know about yourself... but you need to do the work!

You may find this hard to begin with as we don't always give ourselves permission to say what we are really thinking and feeling. We may believe it is inappropriate to think those things; that we are being silly, unrealistic and immature. Let me reassure you – you are not! These ideas and thoughts are your starting points, giving you lots of information to work with. One 'silly' idea can lead to many other thoughts and ideas that could just unlock that career goal. It is therefore vital for you to be completely honest with yourself, if you are to uncover what you **really** want to do. It is only then that you will have the drive and motivation to truly succeed. If you are not open and honest with yourself, this booklet will not work for you.

What are you thinking right now?

Are you ready to get started?

Don't worry if you aren't! This may not be the right time for you and if you continue, you may run the risk of not being open and honest with yourself and end up feeling frustrated. Leave the booklet for a while and come back to it when you feel it is the right time for you.

If you are ready, then to get the best from this booklet I recommend that you:

- give yourself permission to say and write down what you really think and feel no matter how silly it seems... It isn't!

- be honest with yourself. No-one else has to see what you have written down

- use the workbook in a way that best suits you. You can work through it in order or you can just dip into those exercises and chapters that you feel will work for you. But a word of caution; we often avoid doing those things that are exactly what we need to do!

- talk to people who know you well and who you trust to give you honest, helpful feedback especially when exploring your values and drivers

- avoid negative people; they will only undermine you

- think outside the box... Go back to old jobs, look at your hobbies past and present, think about all that you do, not just what you are being paid to do. Go back to your childhood and think about what you enjoyed back then, your dreams and aspirations

- get out there and talk to people who are doing jobs that really interest you and find out what is involved

- most of all enjoy the booklet. It is about your future and what you really want to do. It is about setting off on the road to a fulfilling career. It may be hard work in places but it should also be fun.

My contract with myself:

I give myself permission to be completely open and honest with myself and to write down what I am really thinking and feeling.

Signed. . . . .

CHAPTER 2

FINDING OUT WHAT YOU <u>REALLY</u> WANT TO DO – INTRODUCING THE 6-STEP PLAN

Finding out what you really want to do is fundamental to writing a successful career goal. It is also important to understand why you want to do it. To be successful, we have to be working on our goals for all the right reasons. If we don't know why we want to do something, we will find it harder to keep going and, more often than not, fall short of achieving our goal.

Before we go on this journey to discover what you want to do and why, let me first define what I mean by "career goal".

What do I mean by 'career' and 'career goal'?

We often think of a career as something professional people have. It is a career path or a career ladder that ambitious and/or professionally qualified people are on. They start at the bottom and work their way to the top. In reality, a career is something we all have when we are engaged in an occupation, no matter what that occupation is.

Similarly a career goal can be seen as something that ambitious people who want to get to the top have. We may think that a career goal has to be remarkable and stretching. Actually a career goal is something anyone who is in an occupation can have. It is a statement of where you want to get to and by when. Anyone who wants to achieve something in their working lives can have a career goal.

There are no right or wrong goals. Your career goal is yours and it is whatever you want it to be – not what someone else wants it to be, or what you think it "should" or "ought" to be.

Career goals can also change over time as our knowledge and experience grows. Our lives change and what is important to us changes.

Should everyone have a career goal?

The answer to this should be yes, but there are many people who lead very fulfilling careers and have never written a career goal in their lives. They may always have known what they wanted to do, or perhaps they were fortunate enough to fall into a career that really worked for them, or opportunities have arisen that have kept them motivated and interested along the years.

However, we are all different and career goals are great if:

- you haven't a clue what direction you want your career to go in, and you want some direction and clarity

- you are someone who likes to know where you are going and what you need to do to get there

- you like structure

- you want to have more certainty and clarity about your future

- you want to be more in control of your career

- you want to be sure you are going to achieve your career ambitions!

Without a career goal you may miss opportunities, stagnate where you are, or wander aimlessly from job application to job application, ending up in a role that you are unhappy in; out of one frying pan into another! You may be lucky and inadvertently end up in something that works for you, but wouldn't it be great to get there sooner? You need a career goal.

Introducing the 6-Step Plan

I have developed this 6-Step Plan to defining your careers goals based on my years of experience in helping people work out what they really want to do in their careers. This plan has helped people realise that they can build a fulfilling and successful career. It can help you work out what you really want to do and build your confidence in realising long-held career dreams and aspirations.

The 6 Steps

Step 1
Unlocking
your dreams

Step 2
Identifying
your drivers
and
motivators

Step 5
Stating your
practical
needs

Step 6
Defining your
career goal

Step 4
Finding out
what you are
very good at

Step 3
Finding out
what you
really enjoy
doing

Step 1 Unlocking your dreams and aspirations using powerful career questions

Step 2 Identifying your drivers and motivators through understanding your values and beliefs and the crucial role they have in helping you define your goal. Knowing your fundamental non-negotiable needs from your career

Step 3 Finding out what you really enjoy doing by giving yourself permission to list everything you love whether you are good at it or not!

Step 4 Finding out what you are very good at by including all those things you don't like doing or avoid doing even though you can do them!

Step 5 Stating your practical needs, making sure you are being realistic and honest with yourself about the practical realities you need from work

Step 6 Defining your career goal by bringing all your information, insights and ideas together to start to make your dream a reality

The first five steps will help you think through what you want to do, and the sixth step will help you consolidate what you have learned from those first five steps into a career goal that you can start using immediately. This goal is also used in *Chapter 3 - Getting Real!* and *Chapter 4 - Writing Brilliant Successful Career Goals.*

As we go through the six steps on the following pages, you will find questionnaires, exercises, tools & techniques and a careers checklist to help you gather all the information you need to work out your career goal(s).

Once you have got to the end of the six steps, you will be ready to move on to Chapter 3 where we do some reality checking and start researching opportunities that will refine and finalise your goal. In Chapter 4 I help you write your goal in a way that will really help you succeed.

Now we start the work...

Step 1 - Unlocking your dreams

Our dreams are just ideas waiting to be explored and, as with all ideas, they are a starting place. Your dreams give you lots of clues about what you really want to do with your career. Your dream may be very specific, such as 'I want to be a general manager of a distribution company', or it could be rather vague, for example, 'I want to work with people where I can really make a difference', or it could be something completely different to what you are doing right now, such as 'I want to write'.

This is the time to give yourself permission to say what you are really thinking and feeling. The following 2 exercises will help you do this as long as you are completely honest with yourself.

Exercise 1 - 12 powerful career questions

This exercise is a questionnaire compiled of well-known and powerful career-coaching questions that will help you unlock your thinking and give yourself permission to dream.

For each question, the right answer is the very first thing that comes into your head. Just go for it!

1. What work would you do if you won millions of pounds on the National Lottery? (Assume you must continue to work but not necessarily get paid!)

2. What would you **love** to do if you knew you already had the skills and knowledge to do it?

3. What work would you do if you only had 12 months left to live? (Assume you will enjoy good health until the moment of your death.)

4. Whose job do you most covet?

5. What would you like to be remembered for after you die?

6. Who do you most admire and would most like to emulate?

7. Looking back over your life, when and in what circumstances have you felt most happy and contented? (Look at your whole life and not just your paid work.)

8. What hobbies and interests do you enjoy most?

9. What job or jobs do you wish you could do right now?

10. What do you really love about your present job?

11. Looking back over your career to date, what aspects of your working life have you enjoyed the most and/or felt were most rewarding?

12. If you could write your ideal job description what would you put down?

Review your answers... In what ways could you combine these activities into a new career or into your working life from now on? Turn to Step 6 and write this in your Career Checklist under ' 1 *Powerful career questions*' together with any key themes and ideas you are uncovering from this exercise.

Exercise 2 - Visualise your future

Now that I have got you thinking, take your ideas and put yourself into your future...

If you were to wake up tomorrow and you were doing exactly what you wanted to be doing, what would it be?

Close your eyes and immerse yourself in your ideal job. Stay there and really look, listen and feel your way around... spend some time there...

Then answer these questions:

- Where are you? What can you see? What can you hear?

- What is around you? Who is around you?

- What are you doing?

- If there are other people there, what are they doing?

- What time of day is it?

- What are you feeling?

- What is going on?

Your notes:

Capture your thoughts here and put any key themes you have identified in your Career Checklist (see Step 6) under '2 *Visualise your future*'.

If your answers are clear, that's great... make a note of them. If your answers are a bit vague, don't worry; make a note of anything you have come up with that feels right. It will all help to define your goal.

Step 2 - Identifying your drivers and motivators

Your drivers and motivators are those fundamental reasons why you do things or don't do things. By knowing and understanding what motivates you, you will understand the drivers behind what you do. You will understand why certain aspects of your working life are important to you and **need** to be a part of your career for you to feel fulfilled and be successful.

To help you understand what your key drivers and motivators are, we are going to explore your core values and beliefs. Your values and beliefs are the code by which you live your life and underpin your drivers and motivators. By identifying and understanding your core values and beliefs, you will know what your fundamental non-negotiable needs are from your career.

Your values and beliefs

Our values and beliefs have been developed early in our lives through our parents and guardians, teachers, influential adults and role models, early mentors in education and work, and others who have had a significant impact on our lives.

When our values are respected by others we feel confident and comfortable in their presence. However, when this doesn't happen we can find ourselves reacting in unexpected ways – becoming angry, upset, frustrated, bewildered and so on.

In work, the organisation we are employed by will also have a set of values. These values aren't always the ones that are written up on the wall! The organisation's values are the unwritten code of 'how we work and behave around here'. In addition, the department we work for and the team we work with will also have a set of values that underpin how people work and behave.

When our personal core values are in line with the organisation's, the department's or the team's, we feel valued and motivated. However, when our core values are at odds with these, we can feel frustrated, irritated, undervalued, misunderstood and at the very worst, stressed.

If this sounds familiar, pause for a moment and make a note on the next page of all those things that make you feel at odds with your current job and/or organisation.

Things I am at odds with in my current job and/ or organisation:

1.

2.

3.

4.

5.

6...

Exercise 3 - Understanding your core values and beliefs

This exercise helps you identify and define your values so you can understand them better.

By understanding your values and beliefs you can start to identify what is really important to you in your career and why. You can then start to see what you need from your job and what you need from the organisation and the people in it. You will be able to identify your key drivers and motivators.

Instructions:

It is important that you approach Part 1 of this exercise from a general point of view. This is important because our fundamental values and beliefs are the same in our work and private lives. When you have done this, do Parts 2 and 3 from a work perspective so you can see how your values and beliefs manifest themselves in your working environment.

Part 1 - Identifying your values and beliefs

Use the list of values on the following table as a starting point, and:

i.   highlight any you feel are important to you. Modify them in any way that will make them more meaningful to you. Add any you feel are missing.

ii. then list the ones you have highlighted in order of importance. If you find it difficult to know which value is more important than another, compare them in pairs asking yourself, *'If I could only have one of these two, which one would I want more?'*

A VALUES LIST

Freedom	Personal development – growth	Security
Responsibility	Truth	Individualism
Adventure	Pragmatism	Knowledge
Respect	Energy	Accountability
Power & authority	Understanding	Money
Change	Learning	Wealth
Giving back – helping society	Community	Wisdom
Caring – helping other people	'Waste not want not'	Fitness
Educating others	Directness	Happiness
Arts	Quality of what I take part in	Commitment
Friendships	Democracy	Fun
Family	Ethical practice	Sharing
Stoicism	Self-respect	Stability
'Stiff upper lip'	Honesty	Purity

A VALUES LIST cont

Love – affection & caring	Collaboration	Tranquillity
Health	Working alone	Conformity
Religion – faith	Loyalty	Quality relationships
Listening	Ambition	Challenging problems
Fame	Survival	Recognition
Team-working	Intellectual status	Work under pressure
Excellence	Positivity	Meaningful work
Flexibility	Achievement	Creativity
Others before self	Nature	Pleasure
Fast living	Variety	Efficiency
Altruism	Sophistication	Fairness
Status	Physical challenge	Openness
Persistence in achieving a goal	Leadership	Being heard
Drive	Country	

Part 2 - Defining your top 5

Now that you have ordered them, take your top 5 values and define each one so that you can explain this value or belief to someone you have never met before and they will fully understand it. Use the My Top 5 Values table that follows part 3 to help structure your definitions.

Part 3 - How do you know if your values and beliefs are being respected (honoured) by others or not?

Once you have defined your values, complete the next two columns in the table below. In the first column, state clearly what people need to do and say to demonstrate to you that they fully respect your value; i.e. how they honour your value. Then in the next column, state what people would say and do to demonstrate to you that they dishonour your value.

MY TOP 5 VALUES

Value rating	Definition of my value: *how do I explain this clearly and unambiguously to someone I don't know?*	How my value is honoured: *what I need people to say and do that shows me they respect my value/ belief and will get the best from me.*	How my value is dishonoured: *what people say and do that makes me feel my value/belief is not being respected by others.*
Example	**Respect:** My value of respect is founded on the belief that everyone has a right to be heard and listened to as we all have different experiences, knowledge and wisdom. We are all equals.	I feel respected when people ask for my views and ideas; treat me as an adult; explain their decisions; use body language and behaviour that is inclusive and open.	I feel disrespected when I am told what to do; when I have no opportunity to discuss what is being said; when I am bullied through body language; when people behave secretively or in a clique. As a result I don't want to engage in any conversations; I will actively avoid these people and it can impact on my self-esteem and confidence.
1			

Value rating	Definition of my value: *how do I explain this clearly and unambiguously to someone I don't know?*	How my value is honoured: *what I need people to say and do that shows me they respect my value/belief and will get the best from me.*	How my value is dishonoured: *what people say and do that makes me feel my value/belief is not being respected by others.*
2			
3			
4			
5			

Now review your values and identify your key drivers and motivators. The following questions will help you do this.

- What do you need from your job to meet your values at work?

- What kind of people do you need to work with?

- What do your values tell you about what drives and motivates you at work? These are your drivers and motivators.

- What kind of work meets your key drivers and motivators?

- What kind of work would meet your values?

- How do you need to work to fulfil your values, drivers and motivators?

- What do you want your working environment to be like?

- What kinds of organisations have similar values to yours?

- What does the perfect organisation look like, sound like, feel like?

- What would be your perfect job? List its roles and responsibilities, and its attributes.

- What don't you want from your job?

- What else?

Your notes:

Capture your key drivers and motivators here together with any other ideas and themes you have identified. Summarise them in your Career Checklist (Step 6) under *'3a Drivers & motivators'* and summarise your values under *'3b Values & beliefs'*.

Step 3 - Finding out what you <u>really</u> enjoy doing, and

Step 4 - Finding out what you are <u>very</u> good at

These next 2 steps give you permission to say what you really think and feel about what you do. Again, being honest with yourself is key here.

In the quadrant table a couple of pages on from here, I ask you to analyse what you do. I ask you to:

1. list everything that you **really enjoy doing – your passions** – regardless of how good you are at it. I want you to include everything, whether you are paid for it or not. Think about hobbies, previous jobs, any voluntary work or home projects you have done. When we really enjoy something, we are much more energised and motivated to do it; which means we will keep going even when things get a bit tough, or when we have to do things we don't really enjoy because we know the end result will be worth it.

2. list everything that you **very good at – your strengths**. I want you to list everything, whether you enjoy it or not. Include everything, whether you are paid for it or not. As in 1 above, think about all the things you do outside work too. You may find this list repeats things from the first quadrant. Repetition is good; this means you are starting to match things up, helping you to make decisions about your career and develop action plans.

3. list all those things that you **really dislike doing** – and I mean REALLY dislike doing – even if you are really good at them. I call these **your avoidances** because if we could, we would avoid doing them! This can often be hard to do, especially if you or people close to you have invested time and money in those achievements. I still want you to list them, though. If we do things because we "ought" to or "should", we are not doing them for the right reasons. As a result, we will find it

harder to energise and motivate ourselves to do them. When things get a bit tough, we will find it even harder to get on and do our work. This can lead to stress and unhappiness, which is not good for you, for those around you or for the organisation! Be honest with yourself and list them!

4. list all those things that you are **not so good at – your weaknesses**; i.e., those things that you and others would consider to be your weaknesses. This is important if you want to make your dreams a reality. There may be things that you really enjoy doing but are just not good at them. That's okay. All it means is that you need to work out how you can get to be good at them! This is all part of being realistic – challenging what you want to do to make sure it is what you really want to do. It is also part of getting a plan together to achieve your goal.

Getting help to do this exercise

If you are finding it a bit of a struggle to complete the table then the following may help:

- Look back through appraisals in your current and previous roles to see what was said.

- Think back to what your friends and family have said about you.

- Ask trusted colleagues what they think.

- Ask trusted friends (family can sometimes be tricky here as they can have a biased view).

- Sometimes thinking back to school and college days may unearth some long-forgotten skills.

- Reflect on what other people have said about you.

- Write out your key achievements (at work or home), detailing exactly what you did. What did you enjoy? What didn't you enjoy? What were your strengths? What were your weaknesses?

Exercise 4 - Your analysis quadrant

1 What do I <u>really</u> enjoy doing? My passions	2 What am I <u>very</u> good at? My strengths
3 What do I <u>really</u> dislike doing? My avoidances	4 What am I <u>not</u> so good at? My weaknesses

Now that you have come to the end of your analysis, take some time to reflect on your findings and answer the following questions:

- What do you want in your job?

- What don't you want in your job?

- What skills do you need to develop?

- What do you need to explore more?

Your notes:

Once you have completed the exercise, review the table for any key areas to be included in your Career Checklist (Step 6) under '4 *Your analysis quadrant*'.

Step 5 - Stating your practical needs

This step brings reality into the process.

It is important to be realistic and for you to be open and honest with yourself about your practical needs both now and in the future. These needs will be the boundaries within which your goal will need to work.

Exercise 5 below consists of a number of questions that will help you think through your practical needs. This is not an exhaustive list of questions and there may be questions that you need to ask yourself that you should add to the list.

Excercise 5 - Your practical realities

What do you need?

NOW?   NEXT?   IN THE FUTURE?

- How important is money?

- What salary do you need right now?

- What salary are you looking for in the future?

- What about the benefits? Life assurance, pensions, holidays, private health care, etc.

- What are your family needs now, next, in the future?

- How many hours a week do you want to work?

- Do you need flexible working hours?

- Do you need to work part-time?

- What about unusual working hours? Shift work, night work, evening work?

- Where do you need to be located now?

- Where do you want to be located next and in the future?

- How far are you willing to commute to work?

- Would you consider relocating for the right job?

- How family-friendly does your next role need to be?

- Other requirements?

Your notes:

Add your key points to your Career Checklist (Step 6) under '*5 Practical realities*'.

Step 6 - Defining your career goal

Your Careers Checklist is now full of all your information, thoughts and ideas from Steps 1 to 5 and now, using the approach outlined at the end of the checklist, it is time to start making your dream career a reality. Review your checklist and bring all your information, insights and ideas together into a first-draft goal or goals.

Your career checklist

Exercise	Key themes	Job/Career ideas and information	Research and actions
1 Powerful career questions			

Exercise	Key themes	Job/Career ideas and information	Research and actions
2 Visualise your future			
3a Drivers & motivators			

Exercise	Key themes	Job/Career ideas and information	Research and actions
3b Values & beliefs			
4 Your analysis quadrant			

Exercise	Key themes	Job/Career ideas and information	Research and actions
5 Practical realities			
Other thoughts, ideas, insights			

Writing your draft career goal or goals

First, review everything in your checklist and, listening to your inner voice, write down your career goal or goals **believing you can have exactly what you want without risk or limitation.**

Your goal or goals may be a series of bullet points at this stage, stating exactly what you want from your career and/or job. This is okay because in Chapter 4, using well-formed outcomes and SMART techniques, I will help you shape it into a coherent statement. You may also find you have more than one goal. This is okay too.

Then I want you to think through the priority of each of the things you have listed. How important are they to you and when do you want to have them by? Priorities will be high (a must-have), medium (highly desirable) or low (desirable but not a deal breaker).

What do you want?	Priority

CHAPTER 3
GETTING REAL

This chapter is all about getting real and giving you the opportunity to challenge your goal(s) to make it as robust as possible.

In this chapter we:

1. ask 'Is the goal really yours?' You will be surprised at how many of us are actually living other people's goals

2. research your options so your goal is grounded in reality

3. pose 5 challenging questions to those of you wanting to change direction or do something completely different

4. test your motivation.

1 Is the goal really yours?

Having drafted out your goal and before you go any further, I want you to check that your goal is your own. This may seem a rather strange thing to do but it is surprising how many times I coach people who start off with goals that are in fact someone else's!

For example, the power of our parents:

No matter how old we are, the power our parents can exert over us is extraordinary. I have coached many people whose goals are in fact their mum's and/or dad's. Their goal is often something that would please Mum, Dad or both, and they fear that if they did what they really wanted to do they would be letting their parents down. They may even think that their parents will become angry or judgemental, and they want to avoid that at all costs.

Husbands, siblings, friends can all have a similar effect on our goal-setting. So it is really important that you spend a moment just checking that your goal is really yours.

> It is only when we truly believe in our goal that we will be successful. It is only when we know the goal is ours that we will have the motivation, energy and creativity to be successful, no matter how long it takes.

Read your draft goal and listen to what you are saying in your mind. Consider the following questions and if you say 'yes' to one or more of them, then your goal is almost certainly not yours. If you have answered 'no' to all of them, then your goal is your own.

- Do you feel you **ought** to be doing it?

- Do you think you **should** be doing it?

- Whose voice are you hearing in your head when you read your goal?

   - Is it the voice of your mum or dad?

   - Is it your spouse or partner?

   - Is it a school teacher, friend or someone else?

If you have answered 'yes' to one or more of the questions above then you probably haven't written down what you really want to do. You may have dismissed your own goal very quickly and instead written down what you feel you ought to or should do. If you have, **it is time to find your goal. Only then will you have the motivation and energy to be truly successful. Remember you are an adult with a mind of your own**. Go back to the beginning of the 6-step model and this time write down what you really want to do. Give yourself permission to be completely open and honest with yourself.

Managing your feelings

How are you feeling right now?

If you are starting to feel guilty about putting yourself first or perhaps a bit angry because this is all starting to feel unrealistic (after all, *'life is a compromise and we just have to get on with it. Dreams are just that; dreams'*), I want you to pause for a moment and consider the following...

- You are an adult with your own ideas, dreams and goals.

- If you are happy and fulfilled, you will have more to give to others.

- If you start out with your ideal, you will get close to achieving it.

- If you start out with a compromise, you will just compromise further.

- People fear the unknown and the different, and they transfer their own fears and concerns onto us.

- Those closest to us want the best for us, **but** they don't know what that is. YOU DO!

2 Researching your options

You now have your draft goal and the next step is to start planning to achieve that goal. That's great, I hear you say, but how do I go about doing that?

At this stage your goal may seem unachievable, unrealistic, daunting or even a dream. The first step is to ground it in reality. To do this, you need to start researching your options.

Research   Research   Research

Doing research will give you lots of information that will help you:

1. clarify and check the reality of your goal

2. confirm that you really do want to achieve that goal

3. change and tighten up your goal

4. give you the actions you need to achieve your goal.

If you are already really clear about your options and what you need to do to start planning your goal, please feel free to skip this bit.

Research is one of the cornerstones of achieving your goal. Without research you may end up making decisions based on assumptions and not on facts. If you do this, you may miss opportunities; you may end up doing the wrong thing and you may end up doing nothing at all.

- I believe that...

- I think that...

- I assume that...

- I don't think...

- How can someone like me...?

- What makes me think I could do...?

- I can't possibly...

- They wouldn't want someone like me...

- Maybe...

... check your facts before making a decision. YOU may believe, think or feel certain things but you could well be thinking, feeling and believing those things based on nothing at all!

Don't know what to research?

If you don't know where to start with researching your goal, I have made some suggestions below that will give you some ideas of where to start researching your options. Good luck.

If you are looking to change direction, get back into work or want to do something completely different:

- talk to people who are already doing the types of things you are interested in

- find out what is actually involved

- ask them how they got into that type of job

- ask them for their advice

- talk to organisations who employ people doing the type of work you are interested in. What opportunities do they have? What are they looking for? What advice could they give you?

- research job adverts in the areas you are interested in

- find out what skills, experience and knowledge you need for those types of roles

- identify any qualifications you may need for the type of job or the sector you are interested in.

Seeking promotion:

- Find out about the role you are interested in.

- Look at job descriptions.

- Find out as much as you can about your ability to do that role. Look at your appraisals, ask your line manager (if you feel confident of their support), think about any feedback you have been given either formally or informally.

- Be clear about any limitations you may have or gaps in experience. What do you need to do to address them?

- Find out who would be carrying out the interview for that role and what they would be looking for in potential candidates?

- Ask the person you would be reporting to what they would think if you applied.

- Ask people in similar roles what they think.

Retraining:

- Research courses through the internet, libraries, colleges and universities.

- Check what qualifications are required.

- Can your experience replace the need for some entry qualifications?

- How much will it cost and what options are there for paying for it? For example, instalments.

- Are there any grants available?

- Could you do part-time, evening, correspondence courses?

- Are there on-line courses you can do that give you greater flexibility?

- Would your current employer finance your training?

- How long would the training take?

- Can you get work experience whilst training?

- How would you juggle work, family and training?

- What do your family think?

- Can you afford to be without a salary?

- What support do you need to enable you to commit the time to the training?

3 Changing direction - A reality check!

If your goal is all about changing direction or doing something completely different, ask yourself the following 5 challenging questions as a reality check. If at the end of the questions you have no doubts, then your goal is the right goal for you. If you do have doubts, don't leave them; explore them and work out what you need to do to address them.

1. **Are you prepared to take a pay cut?** When changing careers we often start at a much lower level as we learn a new role. Are you prepared for this and how much of a pay cut can you afford?

2. **How comfortable do you feel about starting at a lower level than your current role?** You may have to start at the bottom to learn your new skills and competencies. How does this make you feel?

3. **Are you prepared to do what it takes to make the change?** You may need to take some time out to retrain or get on-the-job experience through part-time or voluntary work. How hard are you prepared to work to achieve your goal?

4. **Are you being realistic about your experience?** Put yourself in a potential employer's shoes. Why should he/she employ you? He/she has to make a practical decision based on your actual experience, rather than on what you claim is your potential. Would you employ you?

5. **Do your career ambitions match your lifestyle?** Think through the practical realities of your career change, such as its physical location, impact on your family, travel, etc. Are you being realistic?

4 How motivated are you?

On a scale of 1 to 10, how confident are you that this goal is what you want to do?

1 - - - - - - - - - - - - - - - - - - 10

If you have scored less than 10, what would make it a 10 for you?

What's stopping it from being a 10?

On a scale of 1 to 10, how confident are you that you will achieve this goal?

1 - - - - - - - - - - - - - - - - - 10

If you have scored less than 10, what would make it a 10 for you?

What's stopping it from being a 10?

If you could have your goal right now, would you embrace it?

CHAPTER 4
WRITING *BRILLIANT* SUCCESSFUL CAREER GOALS

Writing a successful goal could be as simple as choosing a statement to stick up on your wall, put on the fridge door or set up as your screen saver so that it acts as a constant reminder of what you want to do, encouraging you to achieve your aims. For some this may be all that is needed. However, if you feel you need more than this and you want more structure around your goal so you are confident you will be successful in your chosen goal, then this chapter is for you.

In this chapter I look at:

1. how to state your goal in a way that will increase your chances of success

2. how to put together well-formed outcomes, making sure you are fully committed to your goal

3. writing SMART goals for success

4. finalising your goal and identifying your long, medium and short-term aims, helping you plan for success.

1 Stating your goal for success

I want you to read your goal as you have currently stated it. Have you stated it in a way that is 'moving away' from something, or are you 'moving towards' something?

For example:

An **away-from goal** would be: *'I want to stop commuting every day into the city and wasting my personal time travelling.'*

A **towards goal** would be: *'I want to work closer to home with a commute of no more than half an hour each way so I can do more of what I enjoy in the evenings.'*

Research has shown that if your goal is stated as a **towards goal** you are much more likely to succeed as you have a clear vision of where you want to get to. This clear vision also means that when you come up against obstacles, you will spend time getting rid of them because you want to get to your end goal.

When people have **away-from goals** they are less likely to succeed. When we state our goals as 'away from something' we are literally running away from the negative feelings of being in that situation. The moment we start to feel better we often lose our motivation to continue, our enthusiasm and energy levels dwindle and we never achieve our end goal. This is because the negative feelings we were experiencing have lessened and therefore our reason for continuing has lessened or gone away.

So if your goal is stated as an **away-from goal**, restate it as a **towards goal**.

A great example of the difference an away-from or a towards goal can make is when we go on a diet. We have great plans to lose weight but they seem to fail with regular predictability. The people who succeed often have very strong towards goals. Their goals may be for better health, a particular occasion such as a wedding or achieving a personal goal such as running a marathon. Whatever the reason, their goal is about **getting to somewhere**; the weight loss is part of a wider important personal goal. For most of us, our diets seem to stop when that waistband no longer feels so tight, we just haven't managed to lose any weight that week or it has just become too much effort. Our reasons to lose weight are not strong enough to get us through those tough times. We have not set ourselves a powerfully motivating towards goal.

State your goal as a powerfully motivating towards goal.

2 Well-formed outcomes

Below I have set out the questions you need to answer to ensure your goal is written and formed so that you clearly understand what your goal is and how you are going to achieve it.

What do I want?	Can I achieve it?	Is achieving this goal within my control?
State your goal in positive language and in the present tense and be specific.	Be honest with yourself but also be aware of any barriers you are putting up. If it is possible for a human being to achieve your goal, then it will probably be possible for you to achieve it too.	That is, can you personally do, authorise and arrange it? This includes engaging people, buying resources, etc. If you have to ask permission from someone else, it is not until that permission is granted that it is within your control.
Are the costs and consequences of achieving my goal acceptable to me?	**What will the benefits to me be in achieving this goal?**	**Do I have all the resources I need to achieve my goal?**
Include here the financial and time costs as well as the impact it will have on you and others when you achieve your goal.	Are they sufficient incentive for you to keep going towards your goal?	Consider both tangible and intangible resources such as knowledge, beliefs, premises, people, money, etc.
Personal fit	**Effect**	**What does success look and feel like?**
Does your goal fit with your sense of who you are and what you stand for?	What will be the impact on you and others when you achieve your goal?	Immerse yourself in your goal. Visualise achieving the goal as if it was right now. What are you seeing, hearing and feeling?

3 Writing SMART goals for success

Once you have your goal written as a well-formed outcome, the next step is to ensure that it is also written SMART.

SMART is a very well-known model used to write clear, concise and achievable goals. Always make sure your goals are SMART.

S - Specific

M - Measurable

A - Agreed

R - Realistic

T – Timed

Make them SMARTER by adding:

E - Ethical

R - Rewarding

Specific – the goal is clear, concise and easily understood by others. For example, a non-specific goal may be *'I want to be a designer'*. A specific goal would be *'I want a job that enables me to use my creative talents as part of a design team to design household products, where my ideas are heard and respected'*.

Measurable – the way the goal is written enables you to monitor your progress and know when you have been successful. Taking the above example, I have made it even more measurable... *'I want a job that enables me to use my creative talents as part of a design team to design household products, where my ideas are heard and respected. My job* *will be 4 days a week, working within a 20-mile radius of where I live and commutable by bus. It will pay me £20,000 per annum with 4 weeks' holiday and provide opportunities to develop my career.'*

Agreed – i.e., the goal is agreed by all those people who you need to support you in achieving your goal. These are the people who if they didn't agree with you and support you, you would find it difficult to succeed. For example, if you had to relocate, take a pay cut whilst training or needed to work longer hours, whose support would you need to be able to do this?

Realistic – your goal must be realistic and achievable if you are to be successful. Only you will know if this is the case.

Timed – always put completion dates to your goals, as goals that are left open-ended are very rarely achieved. By putting realistic deadlines in place, it helps your inner conscience drive you to success. It also makes everything very real. Once you have set your deadline you can, of course, change it but you will be making a conscious decision to make that change and this process can do wonders for your inner conscience and internal drivers!

4 Finalising your goal and the steps to get there

Now, using the well-formed outcomes and SMART approach, bring together your draft goal(s) from your Career Checklist in Chapter 2 and your research in Chapter 3 and write your dream career goal.

My SMART career goal is...

Next, identify your short, medium and long-term aims to achieve your career goal. Use the following tables to help you write out your plan. Don't forget to make all your aims SMART. I have suggested timescales in the tables; however, some of your short-term goals may be in days and weeks, and some of your longer-term aims may take more than a year. Be realistic about your timeframes but also remember to challenge yourself.

If you don't know where you are going or how you are going to get there, how will you know you are going in the right direction or when you have arrived?!

My short-term career aims to achieve my goal are: (within 1 month)	By when?

My medium-term career aims to achieve my goal are: (within 6 months)	By when?

My long-term career aims to achieve my goal are: (1 year plus)	By when?

"If you don't get what you want it is a sign that you don't want it seriously enough or you tried to bargain over the price."

Rudyard Kipling

CHAPTER 5
MY TOP 10 TIPS FOR ACHIEVING YOUR CAREER GOALS

These are my top 10 tips for helping you stay on track, keep motivated, achieve your goal and have a fulfilling and successful career:

1. Make your goal into a project, create a plan or timeline, and review your progress.

2. Cross off each task as you achieve it so you have a tangible record of your achievements. It feels great to cross things off the list!

3. Celebrate your successes along the way, including all those small ones.

4. Know who and what you need to help you achieve your aims. You don't have to do it all on your own; people like to help. It feels good to be part of someone else's success.

5. Get a support network around you of all those people you trust to give you sound, non-judgemental advice.

6. Remove negative people from your life whilst achieving your goal. You know the ones... they don't have any good or sound advice; they just transfer all their own doubts and anxieties onto you or try to pull you down. They will only depress you and undermine your confidence. Keep them at bay!

7. Always plan for disaster. Then, if it happens it won't knock you off course because you will already know what you are going to do.

8. Remind yourself of why you are doing it!

9. Write out a list of all the benefits you will reap when you achieve your goal and put it up somewhere visible. Read it whenever you doubt yourself.

10. Use visualisation techniques. Put up a picture, or a collage of pictures, that visually represents the reasons why you have chosen that goal and what the benefits of achieving it will be. Put it somewhere where you will see it every day.

If your goal is feeling too daunting, remember you **can** eat an elephant… it may at first seem impossible but by good planning, taking it slowly and taking one bite at a time, the impossible becomes possible!

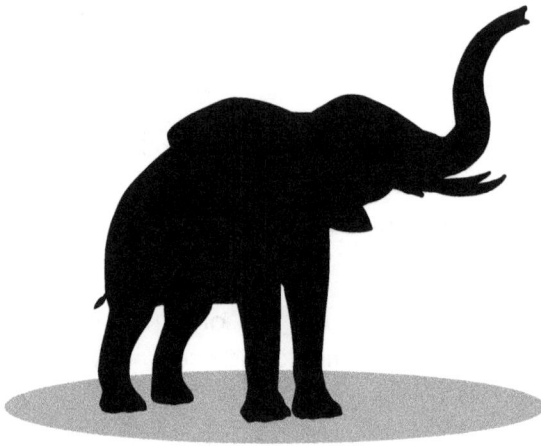

You now have your goal and a way forward.

Take that first step; take that first bite of the elephant, and you will be on your way to a fulfilling and successful career.